ATLAS OF WORLD FAITHS

HINDUISM

Rasamandala Das

A⁺
Smart Apple Media

This book has been published in cooperation with
Arcturus Publishing Limited.

Series concept: Alex Woolf
Editor and picture researcher: Alex Woolf
Designer: Simon Borrough
Cartography: Encompass Graphics
Consultant: Douglas G. Heming

Published in the United States by Smart Apple Media
2140 Howard Drive West, North Mankato, Minnesota
56003

Library of Congress Cataloging-in-Publication Data

Rasamandala Das
Hinduism / by Rasamandala Das.
p. cm. – (Atlas of world faiths)
Includes index.
ISBN 978-1-59920-057-6
1. Hinduism—History—Juvenile literature. I. Title. II.
Series.

BL1203.R373 2007
294.509—dc22   2007007876

9 8 7 6 5 4 3 2 1

CONTENTS

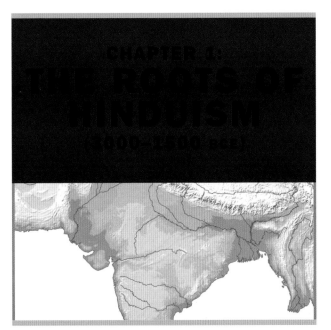

Hinduism is perhaps the oldest religion in the world today. However, it is difficult to say exactly how it started. Unlike most other faiths, it has no single founder, no one scripture, and no commonly agreed set of teachings. Throughout its long history, there have been many leaders, teaching different philosophies and writing thousands of holy books. Because of this, Hinduism is often called "a family of religions" or "a way of life." Its roots in ancient India go back more than 4,000 years. Today, however, large numbers of Hindus live outside India. Many do not even have Indian ancestors, but they have adopted the teachings and practice of Hinduism. So even though Hinduism is connected to India, it is also much broader.

Ancient Indian wisdom Many followers say that their tradition is derived from sacred texts called the Vedas. Veda, an ancient Sanskrit word, simply means "I know." Hinduism does not limit its idea of truth to a single faith or creed but encourages flexibility of thought. To Hindus, being a good person is more important than personal beliefs. Despite this, most Hindus share certain key beliefs, such as the existence of the eternal soul that continuously reincarnates, or passes from one body to another.

In the beginning, these ancient teachings were passed on by word of mouth. According to tradition, they were first written down about 5,000 years ago. However, many scholars believe that the texts are much younger and date the compilation of the first book, the Rig Veda, at around 1000 BCE.

The eternal religion

The Vedas do not mention the term "Hinduism." They speak of dharma, often translated as "religious duty."

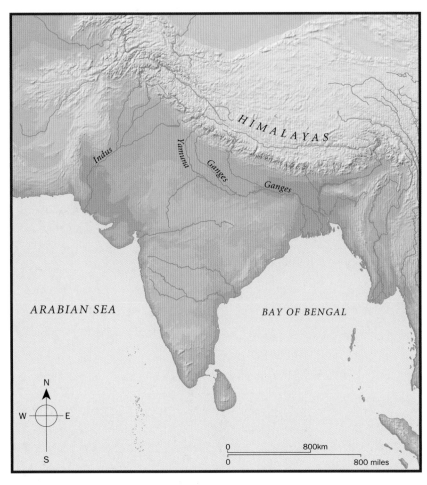

This map shows the geographical features of the Indian peninsula, often called the Indian subcontinent. It is bordered in the north by the Himalayas, to the west by the Arabian Sea, and to the east by the Bay of Bengal. It is most vulnerable to attack through its northwest frontier.

THE ROOTS OF HINDUISM

More precisely, it means "duties that sustain us according to who we are." There are two main types of dharma:
1. Sanatana Dharma: actions based on the eternal relationship between the atman (soul) and God.
2. Varnashrama Dharma: duties according to the specific body we have, determined according to four varnas (social classes) and four ashrams (stages of life).

Many Hindus prefer to call their tradition Sanatana Dharma—the eternal religion.

The creation of the material world
Hindu books, such as the Rig Veda, describe an eternal world made of Brahman (spirit). They also discuss the repeated creation and destruction of this material world. Even after the present universe is destroyed, it is re-created as part of an everlasting cycle.

According to the Vedas, Earth is only one of many planets that exist both in different locations and on different dimensions. Although India is only one place on planet Earth, Hindus consider it special— a sacred land where many saints and avatars (incarnations of God) have lived.

A painting of the spiritual and material worlds. Hindus believe that the spiritual realm is eternal. For them, even this material world continues forever in an endless cycle of creation, destruction, and re-creation.

PRAYER FROM THE RIG VEDA

Om. Oh Lord, the past, present, and future universes are exhibitions of your powers, but You are greater still. The material [physical] creation is only one quarter of the entire cosmos [universe]. The eternal spiritual sky is much larger, making up the remaining three-quarters.

Rig Veda, Chapter 10, Hymn 190

Traditional accounts of history

Because Hinduism's early history is complex, there are many different accounts of it. There are three main reasons for this. First, Hinduism is not a single religion but includes many distinct branches. Second, there are differences of opinion between Hindus and Western researchers. Third, Hinduism has no definite starting point. It is at least 4,000 or 5,000 years old, and it could be much older. To thoroughly understand Hinduism, it is important to study its views on time and its long history.

Hindus believe that since the creation of this universe, time has moved through cycles of four ages that continuously repeat themselves, like the four seasons. Apparently, during the first age—the golden age—people were virtuous and religious. Good qualities decreased through the silver and copper ages until we reached the present materialistic age, called the Kali Yuga, the age of iron. *Kali Yuga* literally means "the age of quarrel."

Two Hindu epics (long poems) give some information on Indian history, although some people consider them fictional rather than historical. The first, the Ramayana, tells the famous story of Rama and Sita, which may have happened as far back as the silver age. The second is called the Mahabharata, meaning "the history of greater India."

The Mahabharata, which was told at the end of the Copper Age, relates the story of five princes called the Pandavas. They were sons of King Pandu and descendants of King Bharat, after whom India is named "Bharatavarsha" (the land of Bharat), or simply "Bharat."

Krishna and Arjuna blow their conch shells prior to the great Battle of Kurukshetra. Thirty-six years later, Krishna's departure from the world marked the start of the current age, the Kali Yuga (age of iron).

KEY HINDU IDEAS FOUND IN THE BHAGAVAD GITA

atman—the real, eternal self, which is neither the mind nor the body

Brahman—eternal spirit, different from temporary matter (*prakriti*)

samsara—the cycle of repeated birth and death (through reincarnation)

karma—the law of action and reaction: good actions bring a good next life, and vice-versa

moksha—liberation from samsara and the suffering it brings

God—perceived in three places: everywhere (as the world soul); in the heart (in humans, as conscience); and beyond the world (as the Supreme Person)

dharma—religious duty; duty in agreement with the timeless laws of God and nature

The Pandavas' cousins, known as the Kauravas, tried to usurp the throne of the vast Indian empire. After many negotiations and requests for a peaceful settlement, the Kauravas refused to give up any of the land they had illegally occupied. Either in support or opposition of the Pandavas, kings from all over the known world prepared for battle on the planes of Kurukshetra, north of present-day New Delhi.

Just before the great battle, Lord Krishna—one of the most important Hindu deities—spoke the Bhagavad Gita (now a key Hindu text) to Arjuna, one of the five Pandavas. Arjuna, though a great warrior, was depressed at the prospect of fighting against his own cousins. Krishna explained all of the important Vedic concepts, starting with the idea that the true self (atman) is not the body. Upon hearing the Bhagavad Gita, Arjuna regained his composure and resolved to fight. He and his brothers emerged victorious, securing the throne of the Indian Empire. Thirty-six years later, Krishna departed the world, marking the start of the present age.

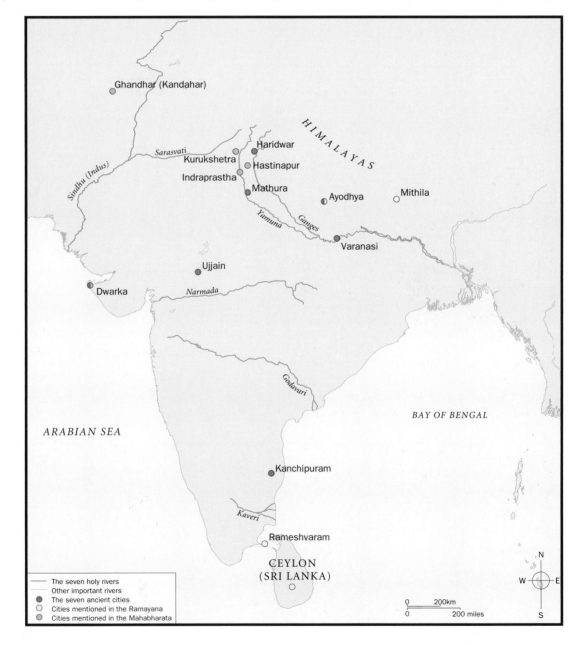

This map shows India's seven holy rivers, the seven ancient cities, and other sites mentioned in the two Hindu epics, the Ramayana and the Mahabharata.

A map showing excavation sites in the Indus and Sarasvati valleys. The course of the legendary River Sarasvati is uncertain, but it may correspond to the Ghaggar-Hakra River (shown above).

The Aryan invasion theory

When Europeans first arrived in India, they knew little of the origins of Hinduism and found very few historical records. They certainly studied religious accounts of history, but they often considered them mythological and, therefore, unreliable. They noted, however, that the Hindu scriptures talked of "Aryans." The Sanskrit word *Aryan* literally means "noble people," but academics suggested that it referred to a distinct race of people. Max Muller, the German linguist, proposed that the Aryans came from outside India, from the west, bringing with them the ancient language of Sanskrit and the beginnings of Hinduism as we know it today.

However, little was known of the Aryan people. Then, in the 1920s, archaeologists unearthed the remains of two walled cites, Mohenjo Daro and

Harappa (both in present-day Pakistan). There was evidence of detailed town planning, with orderly streets and sophisticated drainage systems. The inhabitants even developed what appears to be a form of writing, depicted on various seals found throughout the sites. One seal portrays a figure that resembles Lord Shiva, now an important Hindu deity. To date, experts have been unable to decipher the script. However, scholars were amazed at how civilized the inhabitants had been. Even more surprisingly, they appeared to have lived well before the Aryans. This challenged the theory that the Aryans were the most advanced race of their time.

Ruins at Mohenjo Daro in present-day Pakistan. This site, as well as the one at Harappa, were excavated in the 1920s.

Revised theories Rather than rejecting the original invasion theory, scholars revised it. They now proposed that the Aryan invaders had conquered and destroyed the cities of the much-older Indus Valley civilization. Subsequently, Aryan beliefs and practices blended with those of the local peoples, including the dark-skinned Dravidians (from the south), giving rise to what we now call Hinduism.

More recent finds of artifacts indicate that the Indus Valley civilization was more widespread than first imagined and support the existence of the legendary Sarasvati River (now dried up). This suggests that the river was not a myth, as previously thought, and that Hindu accounts of history can be taken more seriously. However, Hindu texts do not mention an Aryan invasion.

Controversial debates Scholars now more seriously consider the possibility that Hinduism developed within India, and not beyond it. Several Hindu thinkers, and a few Western scholars, have extended these ideas to claim that India is the "cradle of civilization," and not Europe or central Asia, as previously thought. Naturally, some Indian nationalists

favor this idea. The result is that contemporary scholars have started to debate previous theories and often accept earlier dates that correspond to Hindu tradition. However, it is unlikely that anyone will conclusively establish the origins of Hinduism.

EUROPEAN WORDS FROM SANSKRIT

Sanskrit experts have found that many European words come from Sanskrit. Some suggest that words appear similar because both Sanskrit and the European tongues developed from a common "Indo-European" language. In relation to English, the following Sanskrit words illustrate the similarities between the two languages:

Mata—mother
Pita (father)—paternal
Duhita—daughter
Agni (god of fire)—ignite
Sama—same
Sarpa—serpent

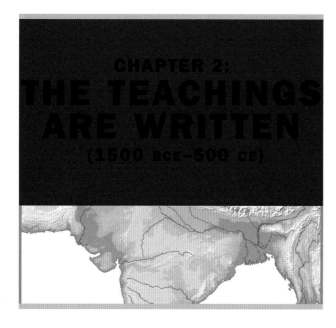

CHAPTER 2:
THE TEACHINGS ARE WRITTEN
(1500 BCE–500 CE)

India's distant past is uncertain. Nonetheless, we know that its ancient wisdom was first passed down by word of mouth and later written. Tradition states that a sage named Vyasa recorded the teachings on palm leaves about 5,000 years ago. Scholars claim that the first books, the four Vedas, were composed more recently, around 1000 BCE. This period, from about 1500 to 500 BCE, is known as the Vedic age. Vedic means "related to the Vedas."

Although there are only four main Vedas, there are hundreds of later texts based upon them. All of these writings fall into one of two broad categories, the Sruti and the Smriti. Together, they are called the Vedic literature.

The Vedas included hymns and chants for use in rituals and sections on philosophy.

The four main books are:

- The Rig Veda – hymns to various deities
- The Yajur Veda – a handbook for priests to use during *yajna* (sacrifices)
- The Sama Veda – chants and melodies
- The Artharva Veda – more hymns and mantras

The main practice during the Vedic age was the performance of elaborate yajnas. The goal was to join one's ancestors in heaven after death. The most popular yajna was the *havan*, the sacred fire ceremony, in which priests tossed grains into the flames as an offering to various deities.

The havan was accompanied by the chanting of mantras. A mantra is a string of sacred syllables. For a sacrifice to be successful, it was essential that the mantras were pronounced correctly.

A painting of a *havan*, attended largely by members of the royal and priestly varnas, or social classes.

THE MAIN VEDIC (HINDU) TEXTS

Sruti: "that which is heard"
- The Vedas (prayers and philosophy)
- The Upanishads (philosophy)

Smriti: "that which is remembered"
- The Vedanta Sutra (aphorisms)
- The Puranas (stories and histories)
- The Epics: (1) The Ramayana
              (2) The Mahabharata
- The Bhagavad Gita (philosophy)
- The dharmashastra (moral codes)

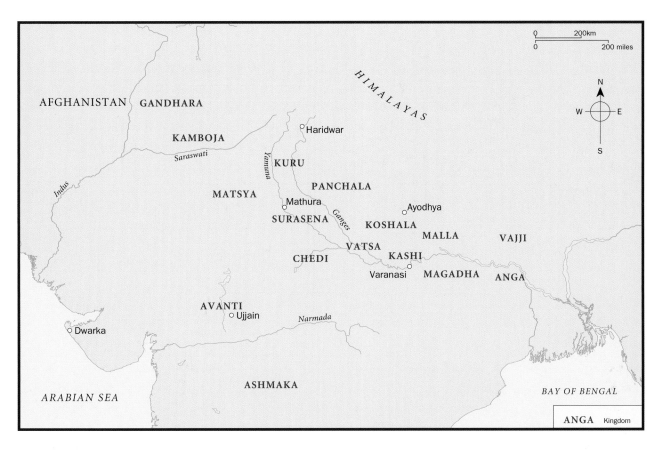

The 16 ancient kingdoms stretched from Afghanistan in the west to the Ganges Delta in the east. Most were situated either around the doab, the fertile area between the Ganges and the Yamuna, or farther down the Ganges, after the joining of the two rivers at Prayag (present-day Allahabad).

The deities The main deities were connected to nature, perhaps because the Vedas emphasized the need to live in harmony with the rhythms of nature, the *rita*. The chief deity was Indra, the rain god, also called "the king of heaven." Agni was also important because he presided over the sacred fire into which all offerings were made.

The main Vedic deities were:
- Indra – god of rain
- Agni – god of fire
- Varuna – god of the waters
- Vayu – the wind god
- Rudra – god of the storms
- Usha – goddess of dawn
- Sarasvati – a river goddess
- Kuvera – god of wealth
- Soma – the moon god
- Surya – the sun god

Books of philosophy As priority was given to philosophical thought, the importance of ritual gradually diminished. Ideas were gleaned from specific sections of the Vedas, called the Upanishads, and were later summarized in an anthology (collection) of aphorisms (profound sayings), now called the Vedanta Sutra, or the Brahma Sutra.

Hindu kingdoms The scholars who taught from these sacred books belonged to the priestly varna (class) and were dedicated to spiritual life. They did not receive wages but were dependent upon the financial support of pious Hindu kings, who were members of the warrior varna. Since ancient times, the warrior and priestly varnas had cooperated to protect and educate the general citizens. By 600 BCE, 16 Hindu kingdoms stretched across the Indian plains, from modern-day Afghanistan to beyond the Ganges delta.

The Mauryan Empire (ca. 321–184 BCE)

Toward the end of the Vedic period, the Magadha kingdom, as mentioned in the *Mahabharata*, rose to power. Since 350 BCE, this eastern tract of land (now the states of Bengal and Bihar) was ruled by the Nanda Dynasty. In 326, Alexander the Great of Macedonia (a kingdom in Greece) conquered the northwestern part of India, defeating King Porus of the Punjab and alarming other Hindu kings. However, upon approaching the formidable Magadha kingdom, Alexander's exhausted army rebelled, turned south toward the coast, and finally sailed westward away from India.

Taking advantage of Alexander's retreat, Chandragupta defeated the Nandas and ascended the throne of Magadha. He resisted an invasion by the remaining Greek forces headed by Seleucus, a former general in Alexander's army. Establishing a long-term friendship with the Greeks, Chandragupta extended his territory to establish the Mauryan Empire, the most powerful empire of ancient India. One of Chandragupta's successors, Ashoka (273–232 BCE), further extended Mauryan territory. Ashoka later converted to Buddhism, ushering in a period of peace. He spread Buddhist ideals throughout India and beyond, even into Mediterranean Europe.

Writings

During the Mauryan period, many important texts were compiled. Chandragupta's prime minister and close advisor, Chanakya, wrote the Artha Shastra, a work that deals with war, economics, and political philosophy. He also compiled the Niti Shastra, a collection of proverbs still widely read today. Many of his teachings were drawn from earlier, oral texts, such as the Manu Smriti (the laws of mankind). The Manu Smriti was also written down around this time, forming

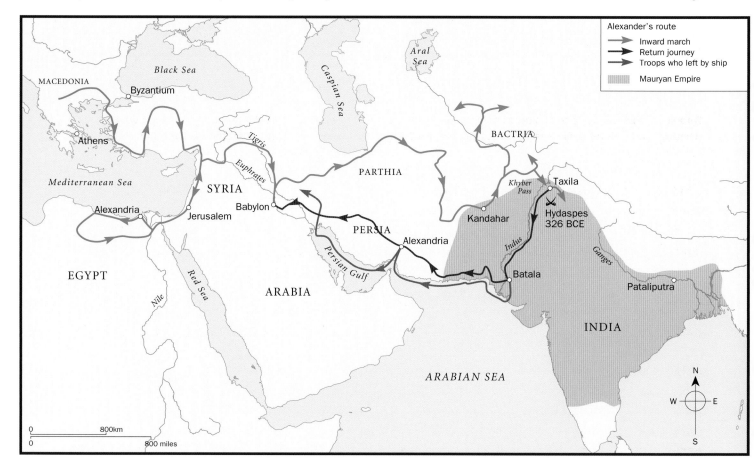

A map showing Alexander's route from Macedonia to India, where he defeated King Porus at the Battle of the Hydaspes. Soon after, Alexander's army rebelled and withdrew from the subcontinent, allowing King Chandragupta to establish the Mauryan Empire.

Temple murtis of Sita and Rama, accompanied by Rama's brother Lakshmana (left) and the monkey warrior Hanuman (kneeling). Between 500 BCE and 500 CE, temple puja became the main method of worship.

a part of the Vedic canon called the Dharma Shastra (moral codes).

Around this time, the two Hindu epics were written down: the *Ramayana*, recorded by Valmiki, and the *Mahabharata* by Vyasa. These works explored the ideal of performing one's dharma (religious duty), and especially the key role played by chivalrous kings and their learned advisers, the brahmins (priests).

Puja Beginning in 500 BCE, the complex rituals and sacrifices, such as the havan, were largely superseded by puja, the worship of sacred statues called *murtis* (see panel). At the same time, the focus of worship moved from Indra and the other Vedic gods, to three main deities: Vishnu, Shiva, and Shakti (the goddess, also called Devi). Later, during the Gupta period, many magnificent temples were specifically dedicated to these principal deities.

THE *MURTI*

The murti (sacred statue) remains an essential feature of Hindu worship. The temple murtis are treated with respect, as if they are great kings and queens. Each day, the priests bathe and dress the deities, drape them with flowers, and offer them vegetarian food and other items of worship. Hindu families often worship small murtis at their home shrine. Sacred texts explain that God—invisible to most of us—appears through the murti to accept the worshipper's devotion. However, for God to be present, these practices must be performed according to strict rules, requiring cleanliness, punctuality, and devotion.

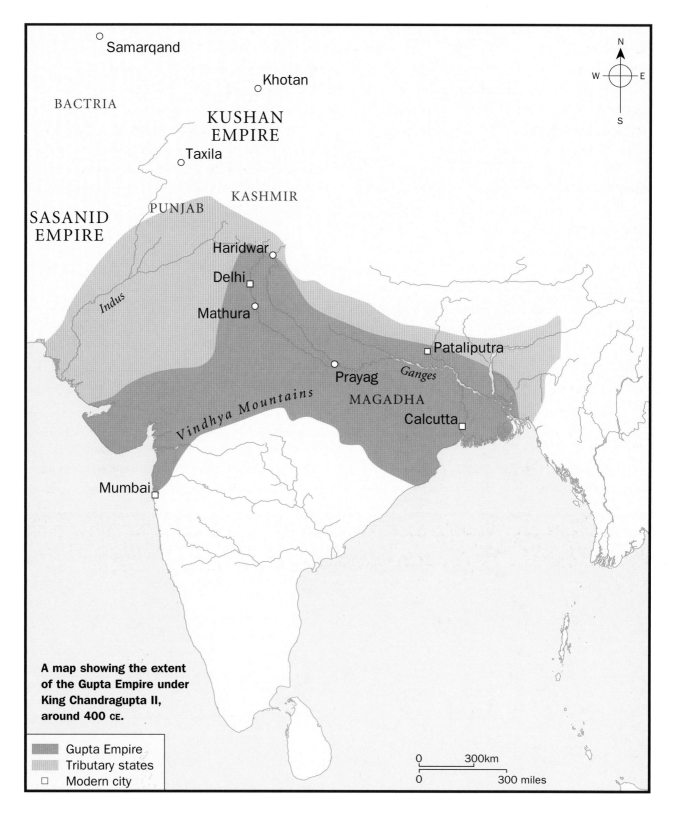

A map showing the extent of the Gupta Empire under King Chandragupta II, around 400 CE.

- Gupta Empire
- Tributary states
- □ Modern city

The Gupta dynasty The reign of Ashoka was followed by a succession of weaker kings and the eventual collapse of the Mauryan Empire. A tribe known as the Kushans invaded the northwest frontier, bringing a period of relative instability to northern India. The Gupta dynasty (320–550 CE) expelled the Kushans and ruled all land north of the Vindhya Mountains for two centuries. The Gupta Empire, though not as vast as the Mauryan before it, left a deep cultural impression on India. Much historical evidence has been derived from coins, monuments, and inscriptions. Travelers wrote of fine cities, well-equipped hospitals, thriving universities, and a population of content, prosperous people. For Hinduism, it was a time of cultural and economic expansion.

Gupta arts and religion

The Gupta period is now considered a golden age of Hinduism, marked by considerable achievement in art, music, literature, philosophy, and architecture. These were largely forms of religious expression. For example, the first dances were not just entertainment but were performed in temples for the pleasure of the deities. With the increasing popularity of puja, many impressive temples were constructed. There is also evidence that Hindu architecture extended deep into Southeast Asia, reaching countries such as Cambodia, where the temples in Angkor Wat were dedicated to Vishnu and Shiva. Within the Gupta Empire, society was divided into different varnas (classes), according to Hindu teachings.

With the rise of temple worship, three main traditions emerged, focusing their respective worship on Vishnu, Shiva, and Shakti. At the same time, the idea of the Trimurti (three main deities) developed. Brahma was considered responsible for creation; Vishnu became "the sustainer and protector;" and the role of destroyer was given to Shiva (previously known as Rudra).

Shiva's wife is Shakti, also called Devi, Durga, or Parvati. Shaktas (followers of Shakti) also venerate the other two wives of the Trimurti—Lakshmi (wife of Vishnu and the goddess of fortune) and Sarasvati (wife of Brahma and the goddess of learning).

The Puranas

During the Gupta period, the Puranas, or "ancient stories," were written down. There were 18 main Puranas, dedicated to Brahma, Vishnu, and Shiva, but with some references to Shakti. The most famous are those describing the activities of Krishna, a form of Vishnu. Krishna is celebrated for his mischievous activities during his youth in the village of Vrindavana, especially for stealing butter and feeding it to the monkeys.

Another popular book, the Devi Bhagavata Purana, tells the story of the goddess Durga. She slayed a demon who took the form of a buffalo. Durga easily defeated him, surpassing the might of all the gods combined.

THE GREAT TRADITIONS

The three main traditions that emerged during the Gupta period were:

- **Vaishnavas**—who worship Vishnu
- **Shaivas**—who worship Shiva
- **Shaktas**—who worship Shakti (Devi)

Later, around the ninth century, another tradition developed. Their followers, called Smartas, worship five deities; Vishnu, Shiva, Devi, Surya (the sun god), and Ganesh (the deity with an elephant's head).

Brahma, though one of the Trimurti, is hardly worshipped at all, except in one Indian town (Pushkar in Rajasthan) and in some parts of Southeast Asia.

Indian dancers perform a dance retelling the story of Durga, a fierce form of the goddess Shakti. Durga has ten arms, wielding various weapons.

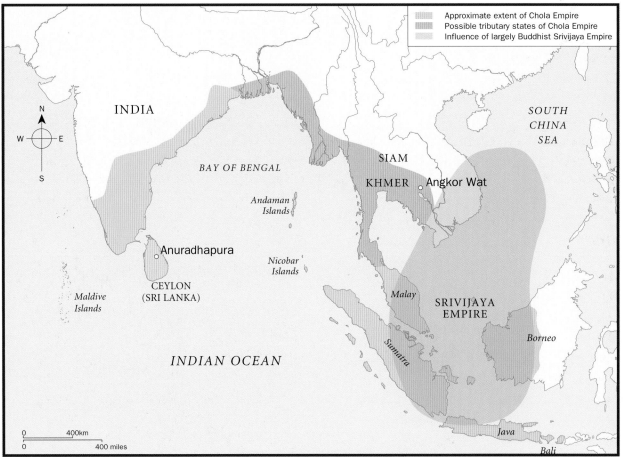

CHAPTER 3:
KINGS, POETS,
AND SCHOLARS
(500–1200 CE)

The Gupta Empire collapsed around 550 CE, largely due to military pressure from the Hunas, or "White Huns," based in Afghanistan. For a brief period between 535 and 700, the Harsha Empire, centered around Kanauj on the Ganges River, united much of northern India and helped resist the raiding Hunas. King Harsha (ruled 606–647) supported Buddhism, and his kingdom was visited by Buddhist pilgrims such as Hsuan Tsang, the Chinese traveler and writer. Harsha was defeated by the Chalukyas, members of a warrior dynasty who briefly expanded their empire to encompass central India.

The Chola Empire (850–1279)

With the fragmentation of the Harsha Empire in 700 and the brief rise of the Chalukyas, power in India shifted southward. The Chola dynasty, which had existed since the first century, gradually overcame the Chalukyas and other southern powers, such as the

A map showing the extent of Chola influence in Southeast Asia. The major temples at Angkor Wat in modern Cambodia were built between the ninth and fourteenth centuries, during the height of Chola power.

A statue of
Nataraja from
southern India.

Pandhyas and Pallavas. At the height of their power,
between the ninth and thirteenth centuries, the Cholas
attacked the Buddhist rulers of Bengal, the powerful
Pala Dynasty. The Cholas were the first Indian rulers to
maintain a fleet in order to extend their territory
beyond the Indian peninsula.

The Cholas were devotees of Shiva but also
supported the other main traditions, Vaishnavism and
Shaktism. They built many impressive temples,
particularly in Thanjavur and in their capital city,
Chidambaram. These temples featured large *gopurams*,
towering gateways decorated with ornate carvings of the
various gods and goddesses. Shiva remained the most
popular deity, particularly in his form as Nataraja, the
"king of dancers."

Hinduism in Southeast Asia

Hinduism may have reached places such as Cambodia as
early as the first century. With the aid of its fleet, the
Chola Empire further colonized countries to the south
and southeast, including the Maldive Islands, Sri Lanka,
and lands belonging to the largely Buddhist Srivijaya
Empire in Indonesia (which included Malaya, Java, and
Sumatra). Chola armies exacted tribute (taxes) from
rulers on the Indochina peninsula, especially from Siam
(present-day Thailand) and the Khmer kingdom of
Cambodia.

Around this time, Hinduism reached the island
of Bali, where it remains the principal religion.
Throughout Southeast Asia, Hindu beliefs and practices
intertwined with Buddhist and native traditions. This
mixed culture still exists in many parts of Indochina and
Indonesia, as evident in the continuing use of long
Sanskrit names.

THE ROLE OF THE TEMPLE

Within Hinduism, the temple (mandir) is
considered the home of God, or of the specific
deity whose image stands in the central shrine.
The main act of worship, called *arti*, is performed
up to six or seven times each day. During this
welcoming ceremony, the priest offers the deities
pleasing items such as incense, water, flowers,
and a lamp.

In the West, temples also serve as community
centers. Some recent complexes have been built in
a modern architectural style, but others conform
to traditional designs, usually drawn from one of
the two main styles, northern and southern.
Northern temples feature a central shrine, a main
spire—and often other smaller spires—and
rounded arches. Southern temples
are often situated in large complexes and are surrounded by
several concentric walls. The
central shrine is reached by
entering towering gopurams
(gateways), each profusely
decorated with carvings of
gods and goddesses.

An exterior view of
the Brihadishwara
Temple at Thanjavur.

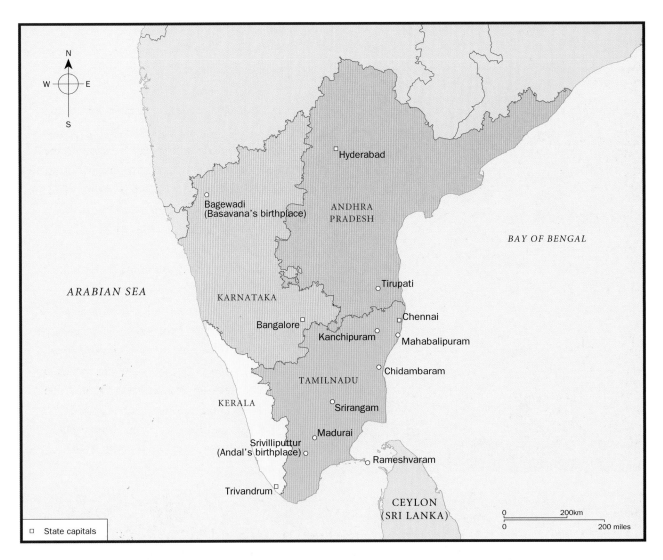

A map of the four states in southern India, showing places connected to the poet-saints.

The poet-saints of southern India

Between the sixth and tenth centuries, poet-saints in southern India helped Hinduism move away from the strict, brahmin-controlled ritual of the Vedic times. Their focus on a personal God laid the foundations for modern Hinduism. The poet-saints wrote in the Tamil language, establishing its importance as a sacred language, much like Sanskrit in the north.

Among the poet-saints were the 63 Nayanars. They were fervent devotees of Shiva and largely unconcerned with philosophical study. They dedicated themselves to practical service, such as cleaning the temple premises, lighting the lamps, stringing flower garlands, feeding the devotees, and performing other humble tasks around the temple. They regarded worship of Lord Shiva's

devotees to be paramount, even higher than the worship of Shiva himself. The Nayanars helped establish the important tradition now called Shaiva Siddhanta.

The Vaishnava (Vishnu-worshipping) equivalents of the Nayanars were the 12 Alvars. Most famous was the female saint Andal, who as a young girl, resolved to accept only Krishna as her husband. She was ritually married to the image of Krishna. According to legend, as the ceremony concluded, she miraculously disappeared into the murti. Andal's life and poetry are still celebrated during a festival that falls in December or January.

The poems of the 12 Alvars were compiled into the 4,000 verses of the Divya Prabhandham, which remains a core text in southern India. It sings the praises of Vishnu in his form as the four-handed Narayan. It is still

FOUR GOALS AND FOUR PATHS

Hindu teachings list four goals for human life:

- dharma—performing religious duties
- *artha*—developing wealth and prosperity
- *kama*—enjoying pleasures of the senses in an ethical way
- *moksha*—gaining liberation from birth and death

There are four *margs* (paths) toward *moksha*, also called yogas, or "ways of linking" to God:

- *karma-yoga*—the path of selfless work
- *jnana-yoga*—the path of philosophy and wisdom
- *astanga-yoga*—the path of exercises and meditation
- *bhakti-yoga*—the path of devotional service; bhakti appears most popular today, though it is often mixed with practices from the other three yogas.

recited daily in the famous Shri Rangam Temple on the banks of the Kaveri River (one of India's seven sacred rivers).

Bhakti movements The poet-saints came from all walks of life and cared little for the Hindu social structure, which by then had evolved into the hereditary caste system. By accepting disciples from all social classes, the saints challenged the authority of caste-conscious brahmins (priests).

The poet-saints gave rise to popular bhakti movements (movements of religious devotion) that later swept north to embrace all of India. One of the first bhakti movements was founded in the twelfth century by a scholar named Basavanna. Members were called Lingayats, after the small lingam they always carried. The sacred lingam is a cylindrical black stone considered to represent Lord Shiva. The Lingayats believed in one God and rejected the Vedas, considering them to be polytheistic (encouraging a belief in many gods). They taught that all beings are equal and accepted women as gurus (religious teachers), which was unusual at the time.

Devotional activities inside a temple in India. The women are praying and making offerings to a large lingam, the symbol of Shiva, while a priest reads from holy scripture.

A traditional painting of Adi Shankara.

Darshan literally means "seeing." The *darshans* are ways of seeing the truth from six different perspectives. Each stresses different beliefs or practices:

1. *Vaisheshika*—the theory that everything is made of atoms
2. *Nyaya*—the practices of logic and philosophical debate
3. *Sankhya*—a philosophy that divides the world into different elements
4. *Yoga*—physical exercises, breathing techniques, and meditation
5. *Mimamsa*—the practices of ritual, such as the havan and puja
6. *Vedanta*—a philosophy concerned with the soul, God, and matter.

Modern Hinduism favors Vedanta but also draws on the other five darshans.

Scholars and philosophers

Around the time of the poet-saints, there lived several key thinkers, known as acharyas, who together laid the foundations for modern Hindu thought. Each *acharya* started his own branch of philosophy. To spread their ideas, they each established a sampradaya, an unbroken line of teachers and students (who in turn would become teachers). The acharyas reinforced the importance of the relationship between the guru (spiritual teacher) and the disciple. For them, knowledge was not merely gathering information but was based on developing character and deep understanding through moral conduct and spiritual discipline.

Vedanta philosophy The acharyas taught versions of Vedanta philosophy. Vedanta means "the conclusion of the Vedas" and is one of the six darshans (orthodox schools) in Hinduism. The darshans are not entirely distinct schools of thought; they represent different ways of viewing the same truth. Vedanta developed two main ideas about God: the first, that he is impersonal, the ever-present world soul; the second, that God is ultimately a person, living beyond this material world. Many traditions combine these two views.

Shankara Shankara (ca. 780–812 CE) was born in what is today the southern state of Kerala. According to legend, he renounced the world at the age of eight to become a sannyasi (wandering monk). He later accepted initiation from a spiritual teacher, who asked him to write commentaries on Vedanta philosophy.

At the time of Shankara, Hinduism had lost some of its appeal because of the widespread influence of Buddhism and Jainism. Hindus had accepted Buddha as an avatar (incarnation) of Vishnu. Nonetheless, many Hindus considered Buddhists and Jains unorthodox for their rejection of the Vedic texts. Shankara traveled throughout India, reestablishing the authority of the Vedic literature and defeating opposing arguments.

Shankara started the advaita school of Vedanta, teaching that the soul and God are identical. He founded a fourth strand of Hinduism called the Smarta school, distinct from the already existing Vaishnava, Shaiva, and Shakta traditions (see page 15). He also

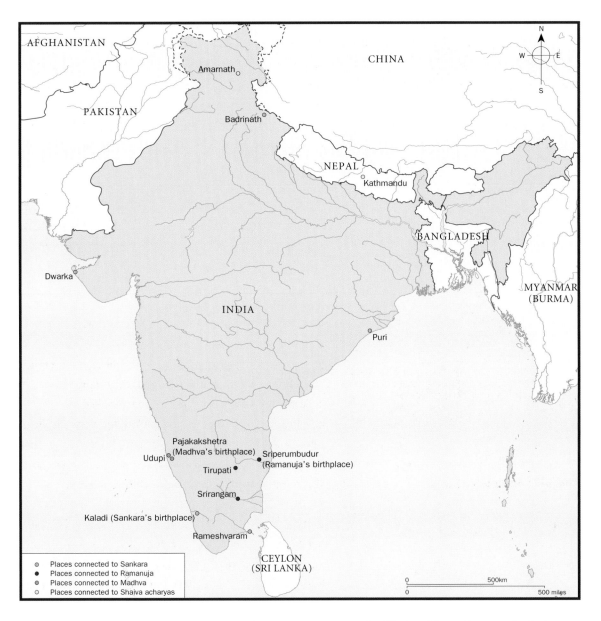

A map showing the cities and holy sites connected to the major Hindu philosophers and scholars.

established monasteries in four places, representing the four cardinal directions—in the north, east, south, and west of India.

Ramanuja and Madhva

Ramanuja (1017–1137) was the most important acharya among the Shri Vaishnava sampradaya of southern India. He extended Shankara's doctrine. For Ramanuja, God not only exists everywhere as a formless energy, as Shankara taught, but is also a person with a spiritual body. Salvation is obtained largely through grace (God's favor), by which the soul (atman) enters Vishnu's house to live forever in a spiritual form. Today, Tirupati and Shri Rangam in southern India remain the main centers of Shri Vaishnavism.

More strongly than Ramanuja before him, Madhva (1238–1317) stressed the personal form of God, as Krishna, and the eternal distinction between God and the soul (atman). The headquarters of the Madhva tradition are in Udupi in the state of Karnataka.

Ramanuja and Madhva were both Vaishnavas. There were also several Shaiva (Shiva-worshipping) acharyas, such as Abhinavagupta, Srikantha, and Bhojadeva, who taught their own philosophies.

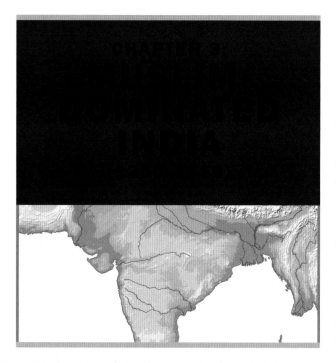

By the eleventh century, while Hindu kingdoms flourished in the south, religious life was threatened in the north. The relatively new religion of Islam had first reached India through traders traveling the Arabian Sea in the seventh century. In the eighth century, Iraqi Arabs occupied the northwestern state of Sind. Steadily, Muslims from Turkey and central Asia superseded Persia as the major power to the west of India.

Particularly brutal were the incursions of Mahmud of Ghazni (971–1030), the Afghan emperor. In raids against the northern states, he sacked temples, plundering gold, jewels, and slaves. In 1025, he flattened the Shiva temple in Somnatha, slaughtering its residents. It is said that Mahmud personally hacked the gilded image to pieces and sent the stone fragments back to his capital, Ghazni, to be set in the steps of a new mosque.

Mahmud seized control of much of the northwest of India, including modern Pakistan and Indian Punjab. The period following his death in 1030 saw the gradual erosion of his empire, when Punjab was reclaimed by Hindu kings. To the west, power was seized by Turks and Afghans based in the city of Ghor. From there, they continued to raid northern India.

The Delhi Sultanate

In 1192, Muhammad of Ghor defeated the Hindu king Pritviraj and overran the city of Delhi. Upon Muhammad's assassination in 1206, his successor, Qutb ud-Din Aybak, established the first Muslim kingdom in India. The Delhi Sultanate refers to various Muslim dynasties that ruled in India until 1526. A string of sultans conquered the whole of India, with the exception of Kashmir in the far north and the Hindu kingdom of Vijayanagar in the south.

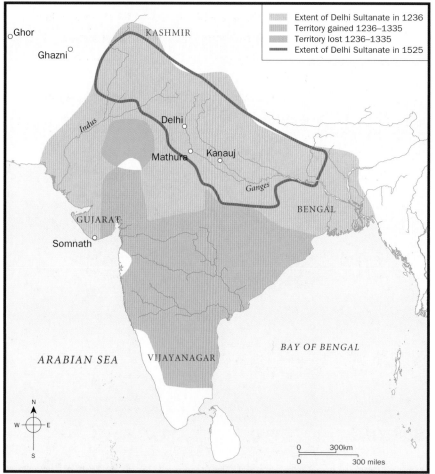

Extent of Delhi Sultanate in 1236
Territory gained 1236–1335
Territory lost 1236–1335
Extent of Delhi Sultanate in 1525

The rise and decline of the Delhi Sultanate from 1236 until 1525, the year before the Mogul invasion led by Babur.

The fall of Delhi in 1192 marked the beginning of more than five centuries of Muslim rule in India. It was to have a significant effect on the way Hinduism developed. Islam was sometimes hostile toward Hinduism, especially the practice of image worship. The ancient tradition of Sanatana Dharma (as Hinduism was once called), well known as inclusive and tolerant, was forced to redefine itself. The ancient Persians had first coined the term *Hindu* in the seventh century, referring to the people living on the far side of the Indus River. By the 1400s, the term had been adopted by those who practiced the faith to distinguish themselves from members of other religions.

The Hindu social system By the time the Muslims arrived, the ancient Indian system of four varnas had developed into the modern caste system. Birth in a high family usually guaranteed a prestigious job. Even if they were highly skilled, those born in lower castes were forced into menial labor. Muslim rule created a governing elite, reinforcing class differences and bolstering the caste system.

Under many Muslim rulers, Hindus were required to pay special taxes. Sometimes they were forcibly converted to Islam. About a quarter of Hindus converted, mainly in the northwest and in Bengal.

Traditional *sannyasis,* dressed in saffron robes and carrying staffs. The Hindu emphasis on personal spirituality helped traditional practices endure, despite centuries of foreign rule and social change.

THE FOUR VARNAS AND THE CASTE SYSTEM

The Rig Veda describes four varnas (social classes):
- *brahmins*—priests and intellectuals
- *kshatriyas*—army, police, and administrators
- *vaishyas*—traders and business community
- *sudras*—workers and laborers

Originally, a person was assigned to a *varna* according to his or her preference for a particular type of work. Later, the system became hereditary, and many subdivisions (*jati*) were added. Today, it is called the caste system.

Dating from the Mogul period, a painting of Krishna and his love, Radha. During Akbar's reign, Hindu art, music, and architecture flourished, but much was later destroyed by the ruthless Aurangzeb.

The Mogul Empire

Due to fierce rivalry between different factions in government, the Delhi Sultanate gradually descended into civil war. In 1398, the capital, Delhi, was ruthlessly destroyed by Timur, a Muslim conqueror who claimed descent from the Mongol emperor, Genghis Khan. The Sultanate never fully recovered, and in 1526, Delhi fell to Babur, a Muslim descendent of Timur from central Asia. Babur subsequently established the Mogul dynasty, which ruled much of India for the following three centuries.

The Mogul Empire reached the peak of its glory (though not its greatest size) under Akbar, Babur's grandson. Born and raised in India, Akbar displayed a positive attitude toward all religions. He celebrated Hindu festivals and began a series of religious debates; he invited not only Muslims but also Hindus, Sikhs, and Christians. He also encouraged members of other faiths to enter his government. During his long reign (1542–1605), Akbar extended the kingdom and left many fine buildings and works of art. He is remembered as the greatest of the Mogul emperors.

STORIES OF BIRBAL

Birbal, a Hindu, was one of the "nine jewels" in Akbar's court. As Akbar's prime minister, he was known for his extraordinary wit. There are many tales about Birbal and how he avoided the intrigues of court rivals. These stories, still popular with Hindus, are often featured in comics and on television. They are part of the tradition of passing down wisdom through stories.

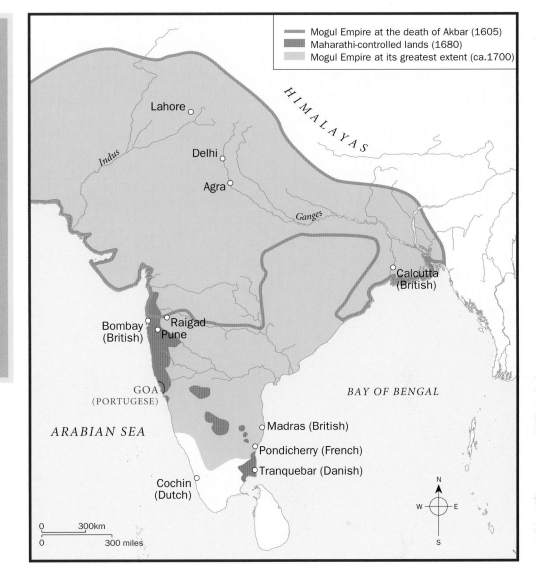

Mogul Empire at the death of Akbar (1605)
Maharathi-controlled lands (1680)
Mogul Empire at its greatest extent (ca.1700)

HIMALAYAS

Lahore

Delhi

Agra

Indus

Ganges

Calcutta
(British)

Bombay
(British)

Raigad
Pune

GOA
(PORTUGESE)

BAY OF BENGAL

ARABIAN SEA

Madras (British)

Pondicherry (French)

Tranquebar (Danish)

Cochin
(Dutch)

N
W E
S

0   300km
0   300 miles

The growth of the Mogul Empire from the death of Akbar in 1605 until 1700. By the end of the seventeenth century, European traders had established several important outposts that threatened Mogul supremacy.

Akbar was succeeded by his son, Jahangir, and then his grandson, Shah Jahan (1592–1666), who was famous for building the Taj Mahal in Agra and the Red Fort in Delhi. Shah Jahan's son, Aurangzeb, was tyrannical, slaying his brothers, imprisoning his father, and proclaiming himself emperor. During his long reign (1668–1707), he discriminated against Hindus, imposing heavy taxes on them and defacing their temples and sacred images. Aurangzeb's religious policies contributed to conflict between Muslims and Hindus in India—conflict that has endured to modern times. Aurangzeb expanded Mogul territory, especially in the south. Upon his death, the Mogul Empire was at its largest, but it rapidly fell into a steep decline from which it never recovered.

New Hindu kingdoms During Muslim rule, two new Hindu kingdoms arose. In the south, the prosperous Vijayanagar kingdom (City of Victory) resisted the military might of both the Delhi Sultanate and the Moguls until its final collapse in 1565. This marked the end of the south as a separate political region. However, a more formidable foe of the Moguls emerged on the western coast of India, in the mountainous Maharathi kingdom. The Maharathi king Shivaji (1630–80) and his successors relentlessly harassed Aurangzeb, hastening the end of Mogul rule. Shivaji was a resistance fighter who exemplified the ancient Hindu ideal of a pious and chivalrous warrior. For many modern Hindus, he remains a symbol of the righteous struggle against intolerance and oppression.

Left: A painting of Chaitanya dancing. He opposed the hereditary caste system and emphasized the importance of developing love for a personal God.

Below: The main states and towns on the Indian peninsula that are still influenced today by four of the prominent bhakti saints and their respective teachings.

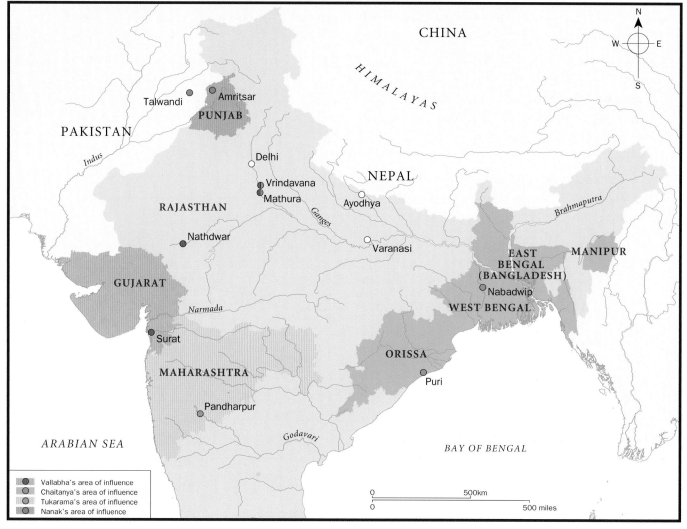

CHINA

HIMALAYAS

Talwandi Amritsar

PUNJAB

PAKISTAN

Indus

Delhi

Vrindavana

Mathura

NEPAL

Ayodhya

RAJASTHAN

Ganges

Nathdwar

Varanasi

Brahmaputra

GUJARAT

Narmada

EAST BENGAL (BANGLADESH)

Nabadwip

MANIPUR

WEST BENGAL

Surat

ORISSA

MAHARASHTRA

Puri

Pandharpur

ARABIAN SEA

Godavari

BAY OF BENGAL

Vallabha's area of influence
Chaitanya's area of influence
Tukarama's area of influence
Nanak's area of influence

0   500km
0   500 miles

Bhakti sweeps India

Bhakti sweeps India The restraints of Mogul rule were compounded by the tight control exercised by Hindu priests. Many of these brahmins insisted on the strict observation of the hereditary caste system, which barred Hindus of lower birth from taking key roles in society or fully participating in religious life. Ordinary Hindus felt marginalized. Leaders arose from among their ranks, stressing the spiritual equality of all and the personal relationship everyone could develop with God. As a result, a wave of bhakti, or religious devotion, swept through India.

Bhakti saints The leaders of this movement, known as bhakti saints, drew on the religious sentiments of the earlier southern Indian poets, and also on Vedanta philosophy, especially as taught by Ramanuja and Madhva. While the earlier poet-saints had worshipped Shiva and Vishnu, the northern traditions focused on Rama and Krishna, two principal avatars (incarnations) of Vishnu. Important saints at this time included:

- Chaitanya, who founded Bengali Vaishnavism.
- Kabir, who taught that God is the same for all, whatever path they tread. His followers included Muslims, Sikhs, and Hindus.
- Vallabha, who favored worship of baby Krishna, a custom that is still popular with many Gujarati Hindus.
- Surdas, who was born blind but became an excellent musician and composed thousands of songs glorifying Krishna.
- Tulsidas, who wrote a popular version of the Ramayana, known as Rama Carita Manas.
- Tukarama, who worshipped the famous deity of Vishnu, known as Vitthala, in Pandhapur (present-day Maharashtra, near Mumbai).
- Mirabai, who is perhaps the most famous female saint within Hinduism.

Music, mantra, and dance Many bhakti traditions popularized the chanting of mantras, either out loud to music or softly on prayer beads. The saints also composed their own songs, poems, and prayers in local languages. The Bengali saint Chaitanya was renowned for chanting and dancing in public. He popularized the following mantra:

> *Hare Krishna, Hare Krishna,*
> *Krishna Krishna, Hare Hare,*
> *Hare Rama, Hare Rama,*
> *Rama Rama, Hare Hare.*

On the other side of India, a Rajasthani princess named Mirabai became renowned for her devotion to Krishna, despite persecution from her family. She finally abandoned palace life to become a wandering saint. Her religious love poems are still recited today. They express intense feelings of separation from God, a mood shared by many bhakti saints.

The birth of the Sikh religion

Guru Nanak (1469–1539), the founder of the Sikh religion, was influenced by the northern bhakti tradition. He taught the importance of chanting God's holy names, as well as the equality of all people and the importance of *seva* (service to others). Nanak's new faith was at first closely connected to Hinduism. Only later did it become a separate religion. Sikhism also took on a military aspect, because its members fought against the Moguls, and later, the British.

A POEM BY MIRABAI

As the whole world sleeps, dear love,
I keep watch, parted from you.
In a palace of pleasure,
I sit alone and awake,
And see a forsaken girl,
with a garland of tears around her neck,
passing the night, counting stars,
counting the hours to happiness.
If I had known
that falling in love
was to fall in with pain,
I would have beaten a drum,
proclaiming far and wide
that love was banned for all!

CHAPTER 5:
BRITISH RULE IN INDIA
(1757–1947)

In 1498, Vasco da Gama became the first European to set foot in India, at Calicut on the western coast. Subsequently, in 1510, the Portuguese conquered Goa. The splendor and wealth of the Mogul Empire also attracted the interest of French, Dutch, and British traders. In 1610, the British East India Company established a base in Surat and other posts in Madras (1639), Bombay (1668), and Calcutta (1690). The administrators of the company signed trade agreements with the Moguls and recruited local men for their own military force. As the East India Company expanded its influence, tensions arose between the company and both local and central rulers, which led to conflict. Robert Clive's victory at the Battle of Plassey (1757) in Bengal heralded the end of the Mogul Empire. By 1769, the East India Company had almost complete control of European trade in India.

In 1857, a rumor spread among Indian soldiers that their rifle bullets were greased with the fat of cows and pigs, suggesting insensitivity to both Hindu and Muslim beliefs. (Hindus believe the cow to be sacred, and Muslims consider pork and other products from the pig to be unclean.) The army rebelled in what has been called the Indian Rebellion, prompting the British government to take full control of India in 1858.

Indian troops on the side of Robert Clive during his victory over the ruler of Bengal at Plassey in 1757.

A map of India in 1857, at the time of the Indian Rebellion, also called the First War of Indian Independence.

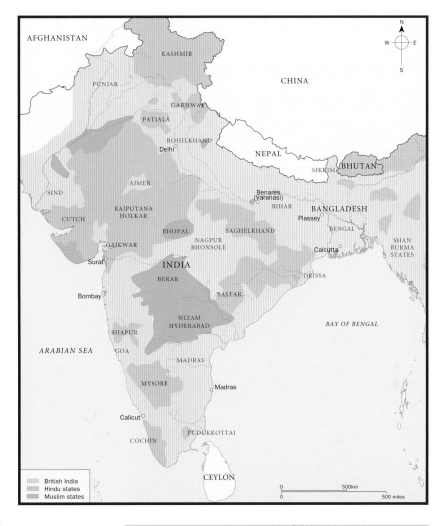

Reform movements

The early colonialists gave Hindus freedom in their religious practice. Later on, some missionaries, scholars, and government officials deliberately attempted to convert Hindus to Christianity, and "civilize" them, particularly through education. These attempts, and the growing contact between Hinduism and the West, spawned various Hindu reform movements.

One of the most influential was the Brahmo Sabha, later renamed the Brahmo Samaj, founded in 1828 by Ram Mohan Roy. Strongly influenced by Christianity, Rama Mohan disagreed with reincarnation and opposed caste practices and image worship. Today, the Brahmo Samaj continues, but with a relatively small membership.

The Arya Samaj was founded in 1875 by Swami Dayananda, who wanted to halt the Christian onslaught and return to the ancient, Vedic religion. The Arya Samaj opposed what it considered later additions to Hinduism, such as image worship, ritual bathing, and pilgrimage. Today, the main form of worship of the Arya Samaj is the ancient fire ceremony.

Reform movements had relatively little effect on Hindu practices, and the main traditions continued to predominate. However, the reform movements did succeed in making Hindus more aware of their unique religious identity. They also gave rise to nationalist movements, trying to rid India of foreign rule. British colonialism also resulted in the emigration of Hindus to other parts of the British Empire.

THE COW IN HINDUISM

The Indian Rebellion started largely through insensitivity to Hindu and Muslim beliefs. Hindu recruits objected that their bullets were greased with lard, or fat, derived from slaughtered cattle. For Hindus, the cow that provides milk deserves respect, much like a mother would. The bull was traditionally used to plough the fields, and it is also accorded a high status. For these reasons, the cow and bull are special to Hindus. Since many Hindus are vegetarian, milk and milk products are an important part of their diet. Ghee (clarified butter) is also important; it is used in cooking, for lamps, and in rituals such as the ancient havan (fire sacrifice).

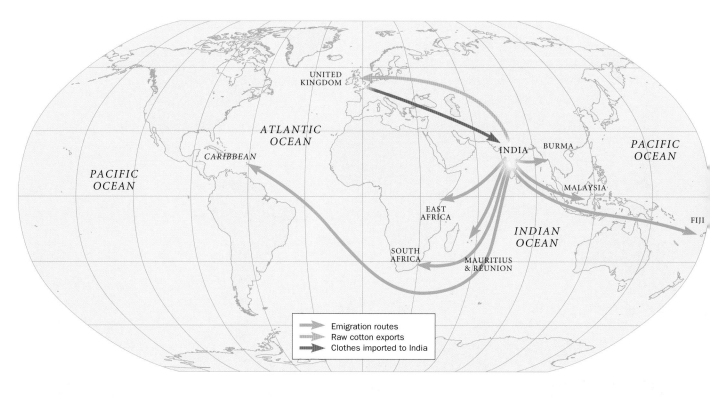

Migration to the Caribbean

Emigration from India had been a continuous process since precolonial times, mainly for reasons of trade. During the colonial period, emigration to the British, French, and Dutch colonies was a means of finding work. By the end of the nineteenth century, emigrants from India numbered almost 1.6 million.

In the United Kingdom's Caribbean colonies, the abolition of slavery in 1834 resulted in a shortage of labor. Western workers were reluctant to move there because they were not accustomed to the tropical climate. Looking for other sources of labor, the colonial governments turned to the 250 million inhabitants of India.

Beginning in the 1840s, mostly Hindi-speakers from northern India were transplanted to the Caribbean colonies as indentured laborers (workers bound by a contract). They were promised fair wages and return tickets in exchange for agreeing to work for a predetermined number of years. Due to poverty, dishonest contracts from employers, and the desire to build a new life, few emigrants returned to India. The first Indians to arrive became laborers for the sugar industry in Trinidad. Others sailed to French Guiana and Dutch Guiana (present-day Suriname) to work on rubber and sugar plantations.

A map showing Hindu migration from around 1840 until the early 1900s.

Southeast Asia and Africa The British took formal control of the western states of Malay in 1870. Many Tamils (from Tamil Nadu in south India) subsequently moved there to become manual laborers in the tin mines, for the railroads, and on rubber plantations. Many also moved to Singapore and Burma (present-day Myanmar). Beginning in 1879, others sailed east to Fiji to work on sugar and cotton plantations. By the early twentieth century, Indians constituted at least half of the population of Fiji.

Indians, many of them Hindus, also migrated to the island of Mauritius, off the eastern coast of Africa, and to the nearby French island of Réunion. Others, largely from Gujarat, migrated to East Africa. Many other Hindus sailed to South Africa to work on the railways and in the gold mines. It was in South Africa that Mohandas K. Gandhi—perhaps the most famous modern Hindu—worked as a lawyer. He was deeply concerned about colonial exploitation and the way Indians were treated as second-class citizens.

MIGRATION AND HINDU CULTURE

Emigration affected Hindu practice, because emigrants adopted cultural habits from their host communities. Hindus abroad—especially men—often began to wear Western clothes. They changed eating habits, sometimes abandoning the traditional vegetarian diet. However, in some instances, Hindus living outside India became more serious about passing on their religion and culture to future generations. As with all religions, it was a struggle to maintain tradition, while at the same time adjusting to new cultures.

Indian nationalism Gandhi objected to raw Indian cotton being sent to the UK, and then clothing was imported back to India at inflated prices. Gandhi personally boycotted cloth that was milled in Western factories. His struggle for fair trade was part of a growing nationalist movement calling for an end to British rule in India and to colonial exploitation.

A Hindu wedding in Trinidad and Tobago. The bride wears the traditional red and gold *saree*, and the groom is in white silk with a decorative turban.

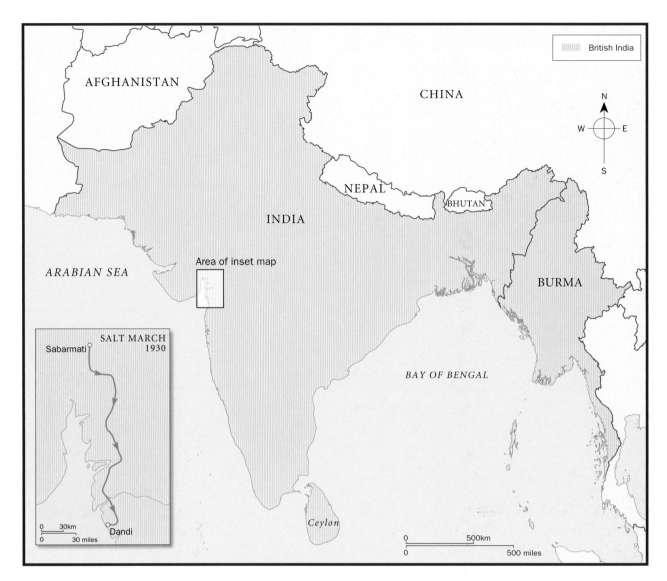

A map showing the extent of India under British rule (1945). The inset map shows Gandhi's route during the salt march of 1930, a key event in the Quit India movement.

Discontent with British rule and the resultant reform movements gave rise to various nationalist organizations. These paved the way for India's independence, as well as its tragic partition. Since independence, nationalist sentiment has continued to play a significant role in the ongoing development of Hinduism.

Hindutva In 1909, leading members of the Arya Samaj founded the Hindu Mahasabha (the Great Hindu Assembly) to give Hindus a distinct political voice. The Mahasabha declared Hindustan (India) to be "the land of the Hindus" and demanded government according to Hindu law. In 1923, Vir Savarkar, leader of the

Mahasabha, coined the term *Hindutva*. It has been translated as "Hinduness." It now largely refers to organizations that advocate Hindu nationalism. These movements include the Rashtriya Swayamsevak Sangh (RSS), established in 1925, which is perhaps the most powerful Hindu organization with around five million members worldwide.

Gandhi's movement Demands for independence increased tensions between Hindus and Muslims. For the minority Muslim community, the prospect of a Hindu government did not seem much better than British rule. In 1915, Gandhi stepped onto

HINDU VALUES

Gandhi was an avid reader of the Bhagavad Gita, which lists many desirable human values, such as:

- Nonviolence to all (ahimsa)
- Respect for all living beings
- Humility
- Mind and sense control
- Detachment from possessions
- Service (*seva*) to God and to others
- Sustainability (*sattva*)
- Cleanliness and truthfulness

According to the Bhagavad Gita, without such values, individuals and societies cannot be peaceful or happy. Gandhi emphasized nonviolence, based on the belief in the soul's presence in all life-forms. For this same reason, many Hindus practice vegetarianism.

the political stage, calling for unity between the two groups. Gandhi led by example. He and many of his followers wore only homespun cotton, intent on undermining the British textile industry, based in the UK. In 1930, he organized a 238-mile (384 km) march to the sea, where demonstrators illegally made their own salt, protesting the British salt tax. In all these endeavors, Gandhi insisted on nonviolent resistance, even in the face of aggression.

Gandhi and caste
Gandhi drew much of his strength and conviction from the Hindu teachings. However, like the bhakti saints before him, he objected to the hereditary caste system. By his time, some people had been labeled as outcasts or "untouchables," indicating a status even lower than the fourth varna, the sudras (workers). Untouchables were allocated only the lowliest jobs, such as street cleaning or working with leather. They were often banned from eating with others, entering temples, and drawing water from village wells. Gandhi renamed the untouchables Harijans, "the children of God."

For practical purposes, Gandhi believed in the system of four *varnas* but not in the hereditary system, which denied equal opportunity. He wanted to incorporate the Harijans within the fourth class, the sudra varna. Another reformer, Ramji Ambedkar, disagreed with Gandhi on the future status of untouchables and advocated instead a completely classless society. Ambedkar later converted to Buddhism and became a hero figure for the Harijans, who renamed themselves the Dalits (the oppressed). Their struggle for equal rights continues to this day.

Mohandas Gandhi photographed during the salt march, in which he personally walked the 238-mile (384 km) route.

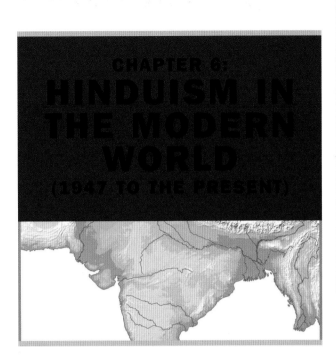

CHAPTER 6:
HINDUISM IN THE MODERN WORLD
(1947 TO THE PRESENT)

Hindus bathe in the sacred waters of the Ganges at Varanasi during a religious festival.

Gandhi led the initial negotiations for independence, which continued in earnest after World War II (1939–45). In 1946, Muhammed Jinnah, head of the Muslim League, declared that a unified India was not acceptable to Indian Muslims, because they were not willing to live under a Hindu-led government.

Partition On August 15, 1947, Indian independence from British rule was accompanied by the creation of a new state, Pakistan, which included two Muslim-populated areas in the eastern and western parts of India. However, partition was accompanied by unprecedented violence. Approximately half a million people were killed as 11 million refugees—including Hindus, Muslims, and Sikhs—crossed the newly drawn borders. To this day, it remains the largest recorded episode of human migration. Gandhi, greatly disappointed by partition and the ensuing violence, was assassinated in 1948 by a Hindu fanatic. His former ally, Jawaharlal Nehru, was sworn in as India's first prime minister.

Bangladesh East and West Pakistan remained one country divided by 994 miles (1,600 km) of foreign territory and by vast cultural and linguistic differences. Feeling neglected by the government in West Pakistan, the eastern state declared independence in 1971, calling the new country Bangladesh. In the following war of

independence, Bangladesh was supported by India. There were reports of further violence and killings, particularly of Bangladeshi students and intellectuals. Bangladesh emerged victorious, and in 1979, it was officially recognized as a new country.

Kashmir After partition, India forcibly annexed smaller territories such as Hyderabad, French India, and the Portuguese colony, Goa. Kashmir, then an independent state, chose to join India, despite having a Muslim majority. Pakistan objected, leading to the first Indo-Pakistan War (1948). A stalemate resulted in a ceasefire and the annexation of Kashmir into India. Religious and political violence continues to this day, threatening the future of a region famed for its natural beauty and rich cultural heritage.

Nepal Although India and Pakistan divided on religious lines, the new Indian government was secular, meaning that it was neutral in matters of religion. After partition, the only officially Hindu country in the world was Nepal, located north of India and south of China. Nepal was declared an independent country in 1923. Today, many Hindus of Nepalese origin also live in the Himalayan kingdom of Bhutan, making up 25 percent of its population.

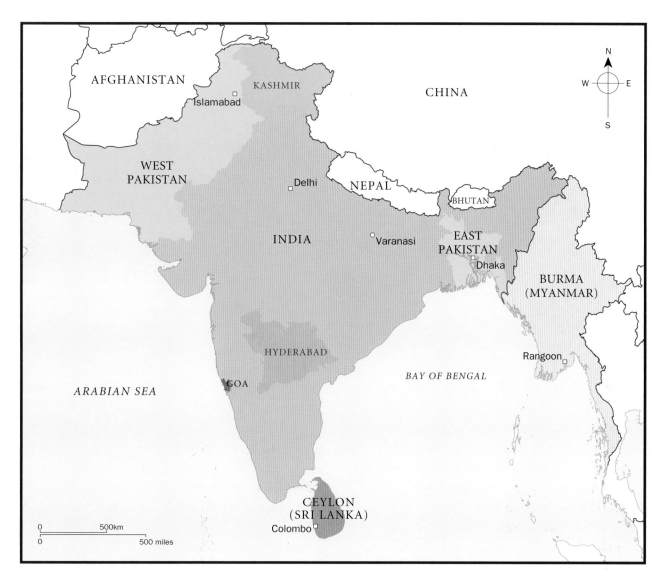

A map showing India and surrounding countries shortly after partition, including some areas of contention. More recently, ideas of "sacred land" have been used to promote Hindu nationalism.

SACRED LAND

While on pilgrimage, Hindus visit what they consider sacred land—sites connected to the lives of saints and the various deities. They take darshan (a spiritual blessing given through sight) of the local murtis, accept hardships (such as walking barefoot), and give to charity. A holy town is called a tirtha, meaning "ford"—a place to cross over to the opposite shore (the spiritual world).

The idea of sacred land has been used for political purposes. Some Hindus argue that the land of India is sacred to Hindus and India should be governed as a Hindu nation. Others claim that the Indian peninsula is special because it is a spiritual place, and it should not belong to any one faith. The precise relationship between India and Hinduism is controversial, especially now that increasing numbers of Hindus were born and raised elsewhere or come from non-Indian families.

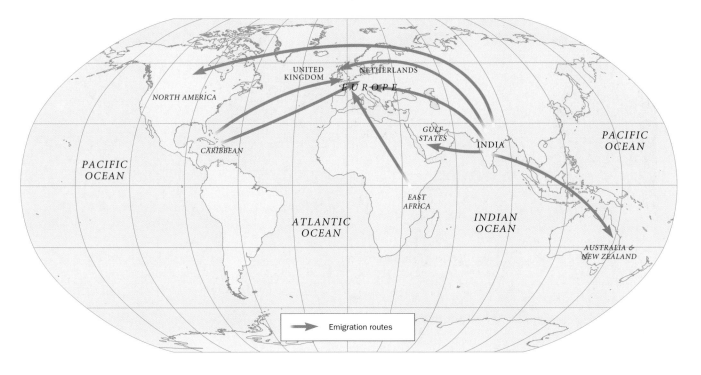

Hindu migration patterns in the latter half of the twentieth century, after Indian independence.

Migration from East Africa

Indian independence heralded the rapid dissolution of the British Empire. Following India's example, many other colonies sought and achieved independence, especially between the late 1940s and the mid-1960s.

In rapid succession, East African countries achieved independence: Uganda in 1962, Kenya in 1963, and the newly formed Tanzania in 1964. Through a process known as Africanization, wealth and position were returned to Africans. No longer feeling welcome, many non-Africans decided to leave. In 1972, Hindus and other Indians were expelled from Uganda, leaving behind considerable wealth. Holding British passports, most settled in the inner cities of the UK. Many took low-paying jobs or started small businesses as grocers, newsagents, and clothing manufacturers. The gathering places for the new Hindu communities were the first Hindu "temples," often converted from old buildings, such as church halls. Here, Hindus practiced their puja, celebrated their festivals, and performed rites of passage, such as birth ceremonies, initiations, and weddings.

The Hindu community gradually established itself both socially and economically. By the end of the twentieth century, Hindus excelled in education and in professional fields. Many magnificent temples replaced the converted church halls, testifying to the growing prestige and influence of the Hindu community.

Migration from India

During the second half of the twentieth century, many Hindus emigrated directly from India. Great numbers moved to North America, especially the United States, where there are almost 1.5 million Hindus living today. Unlike British Hindus, many of these emigrants were professionals, including doctors, engineers, and Internet technology specialists, who sought a more affluent lifestyle. Other Indians moved to Europe, often from southern India and Sri Lanka, establishing the presence of the previously under represented southern Indian Hindu traditions.

Since 1965, many Hindus have sought economic advantage in the oil-rich countries near the Persian Gulf. About one million Hindus now live there, mainly in Bahrain, Kuwait, Yemen, Saudi Arabia, and the United Arab Emirates. They often support families in India; the money they send to India from other countries is worth far more in India because of the relatively low cost of living there.

Girls dressed as Krishna (left) and his consort, Radha, at the annual Rathayatra cart festival in London. Originally celebrated in Puri, on India's eastern coast, the festival is now replicated in cities throughout the world.

CELEBRATING SPECIAL OCCASIONS

Commemorating special occasions is one way that Hindus maintain and pass on their traditions to the younger generation. Hindus living outside India continue to celebrate the main festivals (see page 45) and to observe up to 16 samskaras (rites of passage). The most important are the birth ceremonies, the sacred-thread initiation, the wedding, and the funeral. Each samskara marks a special event in the journey of life. Since ancient times, Hindus have divided human life into four distinct stages, called ashrams, as follows:

1. brahmacharya ashrama—student life
2. grihastha ashrama—married life
3. vanaprastha ashrama—retired life
4. sannyasi ashrama—renounced life

Even today, a few Hindu men leave home to become sannyasis (monks). Some sannyasis travel abroad to train priests to conduct special ceremonies and to teach Hindus how to practice their religion outside India, within another culture.